# Contents

Some words are shown in bold, **like this**. You can find out what they mean by looking in the glossary.

# Meet the chickens

Different kinds of chickens have different coloured feathers.

Chickens are birds. They have feathers, wings, and a **beak**.

Egg

3 weeks

1 day

# LIFE CYCLE OF A...

# Chicken

## Revised and Updated

## Angela Royston

**www.heinemannlibrary.co.uk**
Visit our website to find out more information about Heinemann Library books.

**To order:**

☎ Phone +44 (0) 1865 888066

🖶 Fax +44 (0) 1865 314091

Visit www.heinemannlibrary.co.uk

Heinemann Library is an imprint of Capstone Global Library Limited, a company incorporated in England and Wales having its registered office at 7 Pilgrim Street, London, EC4V 6LB - Registered company number: 6695582

"Heinemann" is a registered trademark of Pearson Education Limited, under licence to Capstone Global Library Limited

Edited by Adrian Vigliano, Harriet Milles, Diyan Leake
Designed by Kimberly R. Miracle and Tony Miracle
Original illustrations © Capstone Global Library Limited 1998, 2009
Illustrated by Alan Fraser
Picture research by Tracy Cummins
Originated by Chroma Graphics (Overseas) Pte Ltd
Printed in China by South China Printing Company Ltd

ISBN 978 0 431 99949 4 (hardback)
13 12 11 10 09
10 9 8 7 6 5 4 3 2 1

ISBN 978 0 431 99967 8 (paperback)
13 12 11 10 09
10 9 8 7 6 5 4 3 2 1

**British Library Cataloguing in Publication Data**
Royston, Angela.
  Life cycle of a chicken. -- 2nd ed.
  1. Chickens--Life cycles--Juvenile literature.
  I. Title II. Chicken
  598.6'25156-dc22

**Acknowledgements**
We would like to thank the following for permission to reproduce photographs: Photo Researchers Inc. pp. 14 (© Tim Davis ), 23 (© Kenneth H. Thomas), 29 left (© Tim Davis); Photolibrary p. 11 (© Oxford Scientific Films/David Thompson); Photoshot pp. 12 (Bruce Coleman/Jane Burton), 24 (© NHPA/William Paton, 25 (© NHPA/Manfred Danegger); © Roger Scruton pp. 7, 15, 16, 17, 18, 20, 21, 22); Shutterstock pp. 4 (© Monika23), 5 (© Elizabeth Dover), 6 (© Smit), 8 (© Saied Shahin Kiya), 9 (© Saied Shahin Kiya), 10 (© MediaForest/Teruhiko Mori), 13 (© Adrian Baras), 19 (© Babusi Octavian Florentin), 26 (© Michiel de Boer), 27 (© Lilya), 28 top left (© Smit), 28 top right (© Saied Shahin Kiya), 28 bottom (© MediaForest/Teruhiko Mori), 29 right (© Elizabeth Dover).

Cover photograph reproduced with permission of Shutterstock (Ronen).

We would like to thank Michael Bright for his invaluable help in the preparation of this book.

Every effort has been made to contact copyright holders of material reproduced in this book. Any omissions will be rectified in subsequent printings if notice is given to the publisher.

The chicken in this book is a white leghorn cockerel. He began life inside an egg. The egg was laid by his mother, a white leghorn hen.

A cockerel is an adult male chicken.

# The eggs are laid

There are nine eggs in this nest.

The hen laid the egg in a nest. Every day she laid another egg.

Egg

3 weeks

1 day

Hens sit on their eggs to keep them warm.

Inside each egg a new chick is growing.

# 3 weeks later

The chick uses its **beak** to chip a hole in the shell.

The hen hears a tiny tapping sound. The chicks are beginning to **hatch** out of the eggs.

Egg

3 weeks

1 day

The new little chick is wet and tired.

The chick chips a hole all around the egg. Then it uses its body to push the egg apart.

# 1 day old

The chicks **hatch** one by one.

Very soon the chick is dry. It is covered in soft **down**. The little chick stands up and looks around.

Egg

3 weeks

1 day

This chick has just hatched too.

Soon all the chicks have left the eggs.
They cheep loudly.

# 4 days old

The chicks drink water and peck seeds in the straw.

The little chicks stay close together. They follow the mother hen wherever she goes.

Egg

3 weeks

1 day

This chick has been left behind!

Chicks that are left behind get scared and lonely. They run after the mother hen when they hear her clucking.

7 weeks

1 year

# 7 weeks old

Big chicks still shelter under this cockerel's wing.

The chicks get bigger. New white feathers grow in place of the yellow **down**.

Egg

3 weeks

1 day

comb

The young cockerel soon looks like an adult chicken.

Cockerels grow long tail feathers and a red **comb** on top of their head.

7 weeks

# 2 months

The chickens leave their mother. They live in the **chicken run** with the other hens.

One of the chickens flies up onto a fence to look around the chicken run.

| Egg | 3 weeks | 1 day |
|---|---|---|
|  |  |  |

The cockerel pecks in the grass looking for seeds and worms.

Chickens swallow their food whole. They have a stomach called a **gizzard** where the food is ground up.

# 5 months

The chickens are nearly full grown. One day a hen sits in one of the egg boxes in the hen house. She clucks loudly and climbs out.

This hen is climbing out of the hen house.

| Egg | 3 weeks | 1 day |
|-----|---------|-------|
|  |  |  |

Hens will lay an egg almost every day.

She has just laid her first egg! It has not been **fertilized**, so there is no chick growing inside it.

# 8 months

If a hen wanders off, the cockerel chases it back.

The young cockerel struts around the farmyard. He watches carefully over several young hens.

Egg

3 weeks

1 day

The cockerel thinks these hens are his.

If another cockerel comes near one of his hens, he chases it away.

# 1 year

This hen is ready to mate.

The young cockerel **mates** with a hen and **fertilizes** her eggs. The hen lays the eggs and sits on them.

Egg

3 weeks

1 day

There are five chicks in this brood.

The chicks **hatch** and there is a new **brood**. The hen looks after them, but the cockerel keeps a close eye on them too.

1 year

# Danger!

This fox has come into the chicken run.

Very early one morning a fox climbs into the **chicken run**. At first the chickens do not see him.

Egg

3 weeks

1 day

The fox runs away with a hen in its mouth.

Then the fox grabs a hen. The cockerel and the other chickens squawk and flap, but the fox jumps out of the chicken run.

# The farmyard

The cockerel has a busy life.

The cockerel watches over the hens and chicks. He will stay on the farm until he dies.

| Egg | 3 weeks | 1 day |
| --- | --- | --- |

From time to time the cockerel crows loudly.

If the fox doesn't catch him, the cockerel may live until he is about 10 years old.

# Life cycle

Eggs

3 weeks later

1 day old

7 weeks old

1 year old

# Fact file

- A hen lays between 100 and 300 eggs a year, but not more than one a day.

- The shell forms around the egg inside the hen's body. It takes about a day for the egg to form before it is ready to be laid.

- People have kept chickens for over 3,000 years. They collect their eggs and eat them.

- Chickens are probably the most common bird in the world. There are more than 10 billion (10,000,000,000) of them.

# Glossary

**beak**  hard covering of a bird's mouth

**brood**  group of birds that hatch at the same time

**chicken run**  area of fenced-in ground near a hen house

**comb**  red crest on the top of a chicken's head

**down**  soft feathers

**fertilize**  join a female egg with a sperm from a male

**gizzard**  special stomach that chickens have for grinding up food before it passes into a second stomach

**hatch**  break out of an egg

**mate**  come together (male and female) to produce young

# More books to read

*From Egg to Chicken (How Living Things Grow)*, Anita Ganeri (Heinemann Library, 2006)

*The Life Cycle of a Chicken (Learning About Life Cycles)*, Ruth Thomson and Camilla Lloyd (Wayland, 2007)

*Where do Chicks Come From?*, Amy E. Sklansky (HarperCollins Publishers, 2005)

# Index